William Watson

Lachrymae Musarum and Other Poems

William Watson

Lachrymae Musarum and Other Poems

ISBN/EAN: 9783744753296

Printed in Europe, USA, Canada, Australia, Japan

Cover: Foto ©Thomas Meinert / pixelio.de

More available books at **www.hansebooks.com**

LACHRYMÆ MUSARUM

AND

OTHER POEMS

BY

WILLIAM WATSON

London

MACMILLAN AND CO.

AND NEW YORK

1892

TO

RICHARD HOLT HUTTON

AND

MEREDITH TOWNSEND

WITH GRATITUDE

CONTENTS

LACHRYMÆ MUSARUM

(6TH OCTOBER 1892)

LOW, like another's, lies the laurelled head :

The life that seemed a perfect song is o'er :

Carry the last great bard to his last bed.

Land that he loved, thy noblest voice is mute.

Land that he loved, that loved him ! nevermore

Meadow of thine, smooth lawn or wild sea-shore,

Gardens of odorous bloom and tremulous fruit,

Or woodlands old, like Druid couches spread,

The master's feet shall tread.

B

Death's little rift hath rent the faultless lute :
The singer of undying songs is dead.

Lo, in this season pensive-hued and grave,
While fades and falls the doomed, reluctant
    leaf
From withered Earth's fantastic coronal,
With wandering sighs of forest and of wave
Mingles the murmur of a people's grief
For him whose leaf shall fade not, neither fall.
He hath fared forth, beyond these suns and
    showers.
For us, the autumn glow, the autumn flame,
And soon the winter silence shall be ours :
Him the eternal spring of fadeless fame
Crowns with no mortal flowers.

Rapt though he be from us,

Virgil salutes him, and Theocritus ;

Catullús, mightiest-brained Lucretius, each

Greets him, their brother, on the Stygian beach ;

Proudly a gaunt right hand doth Dante reach ;

Milton   and   Wordsworth   bid   him   welcome

    home ;

Bright Keats to touch his raiment doth beseech ;

Coleridge, his locks aspersed with fairy foam,

Calm Spenser, Chaucer suave,

His equal friendship crave :

And godlike spirits hail him guest, in speech

Of Athens, Florence, Weimar, Stratford, Rome.

What needs his laurel our ephemeral tears,

To save from visitation of decay ?

Not in this temporal sunlight, now, that bay

Blooms, nor to perishable mundane ears

Sings he with lips of transitory clay ;　　•

For he hath joined the chorus of his peers

In habitations of the perfect day :

His earthly notes a heavenly audience hears,

And more melodious are henceforth the spheres,

Enriched with music stol'n from earth away.

He hath returned to regions whence he came.

Him doth the spirit divine

Of universal loveliness reclaim.

All nature is his shrine.

Seek him henceforward in the wind and sea,

In earth's and air's emotion or repose,

In every star's august serenity,

And in the rapture of the flaming rose.

There seek him if ye would not seek in vain,

There, in the rhythm and music of the Whole ;

Yea, and for ever in the human soul

Made stronger and more beauteous by his strain.

For lo ! creation's self is one great choir,

And what is nature's order but the rhyme

Whereto the worlds keep time,

And all things move with all things from their
     prime ?

Who shall expound the mystery of the lyre ?

In far retreats of elemental mind

Obscurely comes and goes

The imperative breath of song, that as the wind

Is trackless, and oblivious whence it blows.

Demand of lilies wherefore they are white,

Extort her crimson secret from the rose,

But ask not of the Muse that she disclose

The meaning of the riddle of her might :

Somewhat of all things sealed and recondite,

Save the enigma of herself, she knows.

The master could not tell, with all his lore,

Wherefore   he   sang,   or   whence   the   mandate

    sped :

Ev'n as the linnet sings, so I, he said ;—

Ah, rather as the imperial nightingale,

That held in trance the ancient Attic shore,

And charms the ages with the notes that o'er

All woodland chants immortally prevail !

And now, from our vain plaudits greatly fled,

He with diviner silence dwells instead,

And on no earthly sea with transient roar,

Unto no earthly airs, he trims his sail,

But far beyond our vision and our hail

Is heard for ever and is seen no more.

No more, O never now,

Lord of the lofty and the tranquil brow

Whereon nor snows of time

Have fall'n, nor wintry rime,

Shall men behold thee, sage and mage sublime.

Once, in his youth obscure,

The maker of this verse, which shall endure

By splendour of its theme that cannot die,

Beheld thee eye to eye,

And touched through thee the hand

Of every hero of thy race divine,

Ev'n to the sire of all the laurelled line,

The sightless wanderer on the Ionian strand,

With soul as healthful as the poignant brine,

Wide as his skies and radiant as his seas,

Starry from haunts of his Familiars nine,

Glorious Mæonides.

Yea, I beheld thee, and behold thee yet :

Thou hast forgotten, but can I forget ?

The accents of thy pure and sovereign tongue,

Are they not ever goldenly impressed

On memory's palimpsest ?

I see the wizard locks like night that hung,

I tread the floor thy hallowing feet have trod ;

I see the hands a nation's lyre that strung,

The eyes that looked through life and gazed on
　　God.

The seasons change, the winds they shift and
veer ;
The grass of yesteryear
Is dead ; the birds depart, the groves decay :
Empires dissolve and peoples disappear :
Song passes not away.

Captains and conquerors leave a little dust,
And kings a dubious legend of their reign ;
The swords of Cæsars, they are less than rust :
The poet doth remain.

Dead is Augustus, Maro is alive ;
And thou, the Mantuan of our age and clime,
Like Virgil shalt thy race and tongue survive,
Bequeathing no less honeyed words to time,
Embalmed in amber of eternal rhyme,
And rich with sweets from every Muse's hive ;

While to the measure of the cosmic rune

For purer ears thou shalt thy lyre attune,

And heed no more the hum of idle praise

In that great calm our tumults cannot reach,

Master who crown'st our immelodious days

With flower of perfect speech.

DEDICATION OF
"THE DREAM OF MAN"

TO LONDON, MY HOSTESS

CITY that waitest to be sung,—

    For whom no hand

To mighty strains the lyre hath strung

    In all this land,

Though mightier theme the mightiest ones

    Sang not of old,

The thrice three sisters' godlike sons

    With lips of gold,—

Till greater voice thy greatness sing

In loftier times,

Suffer an alien muse to bring

Her votive rhymes.

Yes, alien in thy midst am I,

Not of thy brood ;

The nursling of a norland sky

Of rougher mood :

To me, thy tarrying guest, to me,

'Mid thy loud hum,

Strayed visions of the moor or sea

Tormenting come.

Above the thunder of the wheels

That hurry by,

From lapping of lone waves there steals

A far-sent sigh ;

And many a dream-reared mountain crest

    My feet have trod,

There where thy Minster in the West

    Gropes toward God.

Yet, from thy presence if I go,

    By woodlands deep

Or ocean-fringes, thou, I know,

    Wilt haunt my sleep ;

Thy restless tides of life will foam,

    Still, in my sight ;

Thy imperturbable dark dome

    Will crown my night.

O sea of living waves that roll

    On golden sands,

Or break on tragic reef and shoal

'Mid fatal lands ;

O forest wrought of living leaves,

Some filled with Spring,

Where joy life's festal raiment weaves

And all birds sing,—

Some trampled in the miry ways,

Or whirled along

By fury of tempestuous days,—

Take thou my song !

For thou hast scorned not heretofore

The gifts of rhyme

I dropped, half faltering, at thy door,

City sublime ;

And though 'tis true I am but guest

Within thy gate,

Unto thy hands I owe the best

    Awards of fate.

Imperial hostess! thanks from me

    To thee belong :

O living forest, living sea,

    Take thou my song!

THE DREAM OF MAN

To the eye and the ear of the Dreamer

This Dream out of darkness flew,

Through the horn or the ivory portal,

But he wist not which of the two.

It was the Human Spirit,

Of all men's souls the Soul,

Man the unwearied climber,

That climbed to the unknown goal

And up the steps of the ages,

The difficult steep ascent,

Man the unwearied climber

Pauseless and dauntless went.

Æons rolled behind him

With thunder of far retreat,

And still as he strove he conquered

And laid his foes at his feet.

Inimical powers of nature,

Tempest and flood and fire,

The spleen of fickle seasons

That loved to baulk his desire,

The breath of hostile climates,

The ravage of blight and dearth,

The old unrest that vexes

The heart of the moody earth,

The genii swift and radiant

Sabreing heaven with flame,

C

He, with a keener weapon,

The sword of his wit, overcame.

Disease and her ravening offspring,

Pain with the thousand teeth,

He drave into night primeval,

The nethermost worlds beneath,

Till the Lord of Death, the undying,

Ev'n Asraël the King,

No more with Furies for heralds

Came armed with scourge and sting,

But gentle of voice and of visage,

By calm Age ushered and led,

A guest, serenely featured,

Entering, woke no dread.

And, as the rolling æons

Retreated with pomp of sound,

Man's Spirit, grown too lordly

    For this mean orb to bound,

By arts in his youth undreamed of

    His terrenc fetters broke,

With enterprise ethereal

    Spurning the natal yoke,

And, stung with divine ambition,

    And fired with a glorious greed,

He annexed the stars and the planets

    And peopled them with his seed.

Then said he, " The infinite Scripture

    I have read and interpreted clear,

And searching all worlds I have found not

    My sovereign or my peer.

In what room of the palace of nature

Resides the invisible God ?

For all her doors I have opened,

    And all her floors I have trod.

If greater than I be her tenant,

    Let him answer my challenging call

Till then I admit no rival,

    But crown myself master of all."

And forth as that word went bruited,

    By Man unto Man were raised

Fanes of devout self-homage,

    Where he who praised was the praised ;

And from vast unto vast of creation

    The new evangel ran,

And an odour of world-wide incense

    Went up from Man unto Man ;

Until, on a solemn feast-day,

When the world's usurping lord

At a million impious altars

His own proud image adored,

God spake as He stept from His ambush:

" O great in thine own conceit,

I will show thee thy source, how humble,

Thy goal, for a god how unmeet."

Thereat, by the word of the Maker

The Spirit of Man was led

To a mighty peak of vision,

Where God to His creature said:

"Look eastward toward time's sunrise."

And, age upon age untold,

The Spirit of Man saw clearly

The Past as a chart out-rolled,—

Beheld his base beginnings

   In the depths of time, and his strife,

With beasts and crawling horrors

   For leave to live, when life

Meant but to slay and to procreate,

   To feed and to sleep, among

Mere mouths, voracities boundless,

   Blind lusts, desires without tongue,

And ferocities vast, fulfilling

   Their being's malignant law,

While nature was one hunger,

   And one hate, all fangs and maw.

With that, for a single moment,

   Abashed at his own descent,

In humbleness Man's Spirit

At the feet of the Maker bent ;

But, swifter than light, he recovered

    The stature and pose of his pride,

And, " Think not thus to shame me

    With my mean birth," he cried.

" This is my loftiest greatness,

    To have been born so low ;

Greater than Thou the ungrowing

    Am I that for ever grow."

And God forbore to rebuke him,

    But answered brief and stern,

Bidding him toward time's sunset

    His vision westward turn ;

And the Spirit of Man obeying

    Beheld as a chart out-rolled

The likeness and form of the Future,

Age upon age untold ;

Beheld his own meridian,

And beheld his dark decline,

His secular fall to nadir

From summits of light divine,

Till at last, amid worlds exhausted,

And bankrupt of force and fire,

'Twas his, in a torrent of darkness,

Like a sputtering lamp to expire.

Then a war of shame and anger

Did the realm of his soul divide ;

" 'Tis false, 'tis a lying vision,"

In the face of his God he cried.

" Thou thinkest to daunt me with shadows ;

Not such as Thou feign'st is my doom :

From glory to rise unto glory

    Is mine, who have risen from gloom.

I doubt if Thou knew'st at my making

    How near to Thy throne I should climb,

O'er the mountainous slopes of the ages

    And the conquered peaks of time.

Nor shall I look backward nor rest me

    Till the uttermost heights I have trod,

And am equalled with Thee or above Thee,

    The mate or the master of God."

Ev'n thus Man turned from the Maker,

    With thundered defiance wild,

And God with a terrible silence

    Reproved the speech of His child.

And Man returned to his labours,

And stiffened the neck of his will ;

And the æons still went rolling,

And his power was crescent still.

But yet there remained to conquer

One foe, and the greatest—although

Despoiled of his ancient terrors,

At heart, as of old, a foe—

Unmaker of all, and renewer,

Who winnows the world with his wing,

The Lord of Death, the undying,

Ev'n Asraël the King.

And lo, Man mustered his forces

The war of wars to wage,

And with storm and thunder of onset

Did the foe of foes engage,

And the Lord of Death, the undying,

  Was beset and harried sore,

In his immemorial fastness

  At night's aboriginal core.

And during years a thousand

  Man leaguered his enemy's hold,

While nature was one deep tremor,

  And the heart of the world waxed cold,

Till the phantom battlements wavered,

  And the ghostly fortress fell,

And Man with shadowy fetters

  Bound fast great Asraël.

So, to each star in the heavens,

  The exultant word was blown,

The annunciation tremendous,

Death is overthrown!

And Space in her ultimate borders

Prolonging the jubilant tone,

With hollow ingeminations,

Sighed, *Death is overthrown!*

And God in His house of silence,

Where He dwelleth aloof, alone,

Paused in His tasks to hearken :

Death is overthrown!

Then a solemn and high thanksgiving

By Man unto Man was sung,

In his temples of self-adoration,

With his own multitudinous tongue ;

And he said to his Soul : " Rejoice thou

For thy last great foe lies bound,

Ev'n Asraël the Unmaker,

   Unmade, disarmed, discrowned."

And behold, his Soul rejoiced not,

   The breath of whose being was strife,

For life with nothing to vanquish

   Seemed but the shadow of life.

No goal invited and promised

   And divinely provocative shone ;

And Fear having fled, her sister,

   Blest Hope, in her train was gone ;

And the coping and crown of achievement

   Was hell than defeat more dire—

The torment of all-things-compassed,

   The plague of nought-to-desire ;

And Man the invincible queller,

Man with his foot on his foes,

In boundless satiety hungred,

Restless from utter repose,

Victor of nature, victor

Of the prince of the powers of the air,

By mighty weariness vanquished,

And crowned with august despair.

Then, at his dreadful zenith,

He cried unto God : " O Thou,

Whom of old in my days of striving

Methought I needed not,—now,

In this my abject glory,

My hopeless and helpless might,

Hearken and cheer and succour ! "

And God from His lonely height,

From eternity's passionless summits,

On suppliant Man looked down,

And His brow waxed human with pity,

Belying its awful crown.

" Thy richest possession," He answered,

" Blest Hope, will I restore,

And the infinite wealth of weakness

Which was thy strength of yore ;

And I will arouse from slumber,

In his hold where bound he lies,

Thine enemy most benefic ;—

O Asraël, hear and rise ! "

And a sound like the heart of nature

Riven and cloven and torn,

Announced, to the ear universal,

Undying Death new-born.

Sublime he rose in his fetters,

And shook the chains aside

Ev'n as some mortal sleeper

'Mid forests in autumntide

Rises and shakes off lightly

The leaves that lightly fell

On his limbs and his hair unheeded

While as yet he slumbered well.

And Deity paused and hearkened,

Then turned to the undivine,

Saying, "O Man, My creature,

Thy lot was more blest than Mine.

I taste not delight of seeking,

Nor the boon of longing know.

There is but one joy transcendent,

  And I hoard it not but bestow.

I hoard it not nor have tasted,

  But freely I gave it to thee—

The joy of most glorious striving,

  Which dieth in victory."

Thus, to the Soul of the Dreamer,

  This Dream out of darkness flew,

Through the horn or the ivory portal,

  But he wist not which of the two.

D

SHELLEY'S CENTENARY

(4TH AUGUST 1892)

WITHIN a narrow span of time,

Three princes of the realm of rhyme,

At height of youth or manhood's prime,

    From earth took wing,

To join the fellowship sublime

    Who, dead, yet sing.

He, first, his earliest wreath who wove

Of laurel grown in Latmian grove,

Conquered by pain and hapless love

    Found calmer home,

Roofed by the heaven that glows above

    Eternal Rome.

A fierier soul, its own fierce prey,

And cumbered with more mortal clay,

At Missolonghi flamed away,

    And left the air

Reverberating to this day

    Its loud despair.

Alike remote from Byron's scorn,

And Keats's magic as of morn

Bursting for ever newly-born

    On forests old,

Waking a hoary world forlorn

    With touch of gold,

·Shelley, the cloud-begot, who grew

Nourished on air and sun and dew,

Into that Essence whence he drew

His life and lyre

Was fittingly resolved anew

Through wave and fire.

'Twas like his rapid soul!   'Twas meet

That he, who brooked not Time's slow feet,

With passage thus abrupt and fleet

Should hurry hence,

Eager the Great Perhaps to greet

With Why? and Whence?

Impatient of the world's fixed way,

He ne'er could suffer God's delay,

But all the future in a day

    Would build divine,

And the whole past in ruins lay,

    An emptied shrine.

Vain vision ! but the glow, the fire,

The passion of benign desire,

The glorious yearning, lift him higher

    Than many a soul

That mounts a million paces nigher

    Its meaner goal.

And power is his, if naught besides,

In that thin ether where he rides,

Above the roar of human tides

    To ascend afar,

Lost in a storm of light that hides

His dizzy car.

Below, the unhasting world toils on,

And here and there are victories won,

Some dragon slain, some justice done,

While, through the skies,

A meteor rushing on the sun,

He flares and dies.

But, as he cleaves yon ether clear,

Notes from the unattempted Sphere

He scatters to the enchanted ear

Of earth's dim throng,

Whose dissonance doth more endear

The showering song.

In other shapes than he forecast

The world is moulded : his fierce blast,—

His wild assault upon the Past,—

    These things are vain ;

Revolt is transient : what *must* last

    Is that pure strain,

Which seems the wandering voices blent

Of every virgin element,—

A sound from ocean caverns sent,—

    An airy call

From the pavilioned firmament

    O'erdoming all.

And in this world of worldlings, where

Souls rust in apathy, and ne'er

A great emotion shakes the air,

And life flags tame,

And rare is noble impulse, rare

The impassioned aim,

'Tis no mean fortune to have heard

A singer who, if errors blurred

His sight, had yet a spirit stirred

By vast desire,

And ardour fledging the swift word

With plumes of fire.

A creature of impetuous breath,

Our torpor deadlier than death

He knew not ; whatsoe'er he saith

Flashes with life :

He spurreth men, he quickeneth

    To splendid strife.

And in his gusts of song he brings

Wild odours shaken from strange wings,

And unfamiliar whisperings

    From far lips blown,

While all the rapturous heart of things

    Throbs through his own,—

His own that from the burning pyre

One who had loved his wind-swept lyre

Out of the sharp teeth of the fire

    Unmolten drew,

Beside the sea that in her ire

    Smote him and slew.

A GOLDEN HOUR

A BECKONING. spirit of gladness seemed afloat,
    That lightly danced in laughing air before us :
The earth was all in tune, and you a note
        Of Nature's happy chorus.

'Twas like a vernal morn, yet overhead
    The leafless boughs across the lane were knitting :
The ghost of some forgotten Spring, we said,
        O'er Winter's world comes flitting.

Or was it Spring herself, that, gone astray,
    Beyond the alien frontier chose to tarry ?

Or but some bold outrider of the May,

　　Some April-emissary?

The apparition faded on the air,

　　Capricious and incalculable comer.—

Wilt thou too pass, and leave my chill days bare,

　　And fall'n my phantom Summer?

AT THE GRAVE OF CHARLES LAMB,
IN EDMONTON

NOT here, O teeming City, was it meet

    Thy lover, thy most faithful, should repose,

    But where the multitudinous life-tide flows

Whose ocean-murmur was to him more sweet

Than melody of birds at morn, or bleat

    Of flocks in Spring-time, *there* should Earth

        enclose

    His earth, amid thy thronging joys and

        woes,

There, 'neath the music of thy million feet.

In love of thee this lover knew no peer.

Thine eastern or thy western fane had made

Fit habitation for his noble shade.

Mother of mightier, nurse of none more dear,

Not here, in rustic exile, O not here,

Thy Elia like an alien should be laid !

LINES IN A FLYLEAF OF
"CHRISTABEL"

INHOSPITABLY hast thou entertained,

O Poet, us the bidden to thy board,

Whom in mid-feast, and while our thousand
　　mouths

Are one laudation of the festal cheer,

Thou from thy table dost dismiss, unfilled.

Yet loudlier thee than many a lavish host

We praise, and oftener thy repast half-served

Than many a stintless banquet, prodigally

Through satiate hours prolonged ; nor praise less
well

Because with tongues thou hast not cloyed, and
lips

That mourn the parsimony of affluent souls,

And mix the lamentation with the laud.

LINES TO OUR NEW CENSOR

[Mr. Oscar Wilde, having discovered that England is unworthy of him, has announced his resolve to become a naturalised Frenchman.]

AND wilt thou, Oscar, from us flee,

And must we, henceforth, wholly sever?

Shall thy laborious *jeux-d'esprit*

Sadden our lives no more for ever?

And all thy future wilt thou link

With that brave land to which thou goest?

Unhappy France! we *used* to think

She touched, at Sedan, fortune's lowest.

And you're made French as easily

As you might change the clothes you're

wearing ?

Fancy !—and 'tis so hard to be

A man of sense and modest bearing.

May fortitude beneath this blow

Fail not the gallant Gallic nation !

By past experience, well we know

Her genius for recuperation.

And as for us—to our disgrace,

Your stricture's truth must be conceded :

Would any but a stupid race

Have made the fuss about you *we* did ?

E

RELUCTANT SUMMER

RELUCTANT Summer! once, a maid
  Full easy of access,
In many a bee-frequented shade
  Thou didst thy lover bless.
Divinely unreproved I played,
  Then, with each liberal tress—
And art thou grown at last afraid
  Of some too close caress?

Or deem'st that if thou shouldst abide
  My passion might decay?

Thou leav'st me pining and denied,

    Coyly thou say'st me nay.

Ev'n as I woo thee to my side,

    Thou, importuned to stay,

Like Orpheus' half-recovered bride

    Ebb'st from my arms away.

THE GREAT MISGIVING

"Not ours," say some, "the thought of death to
    dread ;
Asking no heaven, we fear no fabled hell :
Life is a feast, and we have banqueted—
    Shall not the worms as well ?

"The after-silence, when the feast is o'er,
    And void the places where the minstrels stood,
Differs in nought from what hath been before,
    And is nor ill nor good."

Ah, but the Apparition—the dumb sign—

    The beckoning finger bidding me forego

The fellowship, the converse, and the wine,

    The songs, the festal glow!

And ah, to know not, while with friends I sit,

    And while the purple joy is passed about,

Whether 'tis ampler day divinelier lit

    Or homeless night without ;

And whether, stepping forth, my soul shall see

    New prospects, or fall sheer—a blinded thing!

There is, O grave, thy hourly victory,

    And there, O death, thy sting.

"THE THINGS THAT ARE MORE EXCELLENT"

As we wax older on this earth,

    Till many a toy that charmed us seems

Emptied of beauty, stripped of worth,

    And mean as dust and dead as dreams,—

For gauds that perished, shows that passed,

    Some recompense the Fates have sent :

Thrice lovelier shine the things that last,

    The things that are more excellent.

Tired of the Senate's barren brawl,

    An hour with silence we prefer,

Where statelier rise the woods than all

    Yon towers of talk at Westminster.

Let this man prate and that man plot,

    On fame or place or title bent :

The votes of veering crowds are not

    The things that are more excellent.

Shall we perturb and vex our soul

    For " wrongs " which no true freedom mar,

Which no man's upright walk control,

    And from no guiltless deed debar ?

What odds though tonguesters heal, or

    leave

    Unhealed, the grievance they invent ?

To things, not phantoms, let us cleave—

The things that are more excellent.

Nought nobler is, than to be free :

The stars of heaven are free because

In amplitude of liberty

Their joy is to obey the laws.

From servitude to freedom's *name*

Free thou thy mind in bondage pent ;

Depose the fetich, and proclaim

The things that are more excellent.

And in appropriate dust be hurled

That dull, punctilious god, whom they

That call their tiny clan the world,

Serve and obsequiously obey :

Who con their ritual of Routine,

   With minds to one dead likeness blent,

And never ev'n in dreams have seen

   The things that are more excellent.

To dress, to call, to dine, to break

   No canon of the social code,

The little laws that lacqueys make,

   The futile decalogue of Mode,—

How many a soul for these things lives,

   With pious passion, grave intent!

While Nature careless-handed gives

   The things that are more excellent.

To hug the wealth ye cannot use,

   And lack the riches all may gain,—

O blind and wanting wit to choose,

Who house the chaff and burn the grain !

And still doth life with starry towers

Lure to the bright, divine ascent !—

Be yours the things ye would : be ours

The things that are more excellent.

The grace of friendship—mind and heart

Linked with their fellow heart and mind ;

The gains of science, gifts of art ;

The sense of oneness with our kind ;

The thirst to know and understand—

A large and liberal discontent :

These are the goods in life's rich hand,

The things that are more excellent.

In faultless rhythm the ocean rolls,

A rapturous silence thrills the skies ;

And on this earth are lovely souls,

    That softly look with aidful eyes.

Though dark, O God, Thy course and track,

    I think Thou must at least have meant

That nought which lives should wholly lack

    The things that are more excellent.

BEAUTY'S METEMPSYCHOSIS

THAT beauty such as thine

Can die indeed,

Were ordinance too wantonly malign :

No wit may reconcile so cold a creed

With beauty such as thine.

From wave and star and flower

Some effluence rare

Was lent thee, a divine but transient dower :

Thou yield'st it back from eyes and lips and
hair

To wave and star and flower.

Shouldst thou to-morrow die,

Thou still shalt be

Found in the rose and met in all the sky :

And from the ocean's heart shalt sing to me,

Shouldst thou to-morrow die.

ENGLAND MY MOTHER

I

ENGLAND my mother,

Wardress of waters,

Builder of peoples,

    Maker of men,—

Hast thou yet leisure

Left for the muses?

Heed'st thou the songsmith

    Forging the rhyme?

Deafened with tumults,

How canst thou hearken ?

Strident is faction,

Demos is loud.

Lazarus, hungry,

Menaces Dives ;

Labour the giant

Chafes in his hold.

Yet do the songsmiths

Quit not their forges ;

Still on life's anvil

Forge they the rhyme.

Still the rapt faces

Glow from the furnace :

Breath of the smithy

Scorches their brows.

Yea, and thou hear'st them?

So shall the hammers

Fashion not vainly

Verses of gold.

II

Lo, with the ancient

Roots of man's nature,

Twines the eternal

Passion of song.

Ever Love fans it,

Ever Life feeds it,

Time cannot age it ;

    Death cannot slay.

Deep in the world-heart

Stand its foundations,

Tangled with all things,

    Twin-made with all.

Nay, what is Nature's

Self, but an endless

Strife toward music,

    Euphony, rhyme?

Trees in their blooming,

Tides in their flowing,

Stars in their circling,

    Tremble with song.

F

God on His throne is

Eldest of poets:

Unto His measures

Moveth the Whole.

III

Therefore deride not

Speech of the muses,

England my mother,

Maker of men.

Nations are mortal,

Fragile is greatness;

Fortune may fly thee,

Song shall not fly.

Song the all-girdling,

Song cannot perish :

Men shall make music,

Man shall give ear.

Not while the choric

Chant of creation

Floweth from all things,

Poured without pause,

Cease we to echo

Faintly the descant

Whereto for ever

Dances the world.

IV

So let the songsmith

Proffer his rhyme-gift,

England my mother,

 Maker of men.

Gray grows thy count'nance,

 Full of the ages ;

Time on thy forehead

 Sits like a dream :

Song is the potion

All things renewing,

Youth's one elixir,

 Fountain of morn.

Thou, at the world-loom

Weaving thy future,

Fitly may'st temper

 Toil with delight.

Deemest thou, labour

Only is earnest?

Grave is all beauty,

   Solemn is joy.

Song is no bauble—

Slight not the songsmith,

England my mother,

   Maker of men.

NIGHT

IN the night, in the night,

When thou liest alone,

Ah, the sounds that are blown

   In the freaks of the breeze,

By the spirit that sends

The voice of far friends

   With the sigh of the seas

     In the night!

In the night, in the night,

When thou liest alone,

Ah, the ghosts that make moan

From the days that are sped :

The old dreams, the old deeds,

The old wound that still bleeds,

And the face of the dead

In the night !

In the night, in the night,

When thou liest alone,

With the grass and the stone

O'er thy chamber so deep,

Ah, the silence at last,

Life's dissonance past,

And only pure sleep

In the night !

THE FUGITIVE IDEAL

As some most pure and noble face,
   Seen in the thronged and hurrying street,
Sheds o'er the world a sudden grace,
      A flying odour sweet,
Then, passing, leaves the cheated sense
Baulked with a phantom excellence;

So, on our soul the visions rise
   Of that fair life we never led :
They flash a splendour past our eyes,
      We start, and they are fled :
They pass, and leave us with blank gaze,
Resigned to our ignoble days.

"THE FORESTERS"

(Lines written on the appearance of Lord Tennyson's drama.)

CLEAR as of old the great voice rings to-day,

While Sherwood's oak-leaves twine with Ald-
worth's bay :

The voice of him the master and the sire

Of one whole age and legion of the lyre,

Who sang his morning-song when Coleridge still

Uttered dark oracles from Highgate Hill,

And with new-launchèd argosies of rhyme

Gilds and makes brave this sombreing tide of
time.

Far be the hour when lesser brows shall wear

The laurel glorious from that wintry hair—

When he, the sovereign of our lyric day,

In Charon's shallop must be rowed away,

And hear, scarce heeding, 'mid the plash of oar,

The *ave atque vale* from the shore !

To him nor tender nor heroic muse

Did her divine confederacy refuse :

To all its moods the lyre of life he strung,

And notes of death fell deathless from his tongue.

Himself the Merlin of his magic strain,

He bade old glories break in bloom again ;

And so exempted from oblivious doom,

Through him these days shall fadeless break in
    bloom.

SONG

LIGHTLY we met in the morn,

    Lightly we parted at eve.

There was never a thought of the thorn

    The rose of a day might leave.

Fate's finger we did not perceive,

    So lightly we met in the morn!

So lightly we parted at eve

    We knew not that Love was born.

I rose on the morrow forlorn,

    To pine and remember and grieve.

Too lightly we met in the morn!

    Too lightly we parted at eve!

COLUMBUS

(12TH OCTOBER 1492)

FROM his adventurous prime
He dreamed the dream sublime :
Over his wandering youth
It hung, a beckoning star.
At last the vision fled,
And left him in its stead
The scarce sublimer truth,
The world he found afar.

The scattered isles that stand

Warding the mightier land

   Yielded their maidenhood

     To his imperious prow.

The mainland within call

Lay vast and virginal :

   In its blue porch he stood :

     No more did fate allow.

No more ! but ah, how much,

To be the first to touch

   The veriest azure hem

     Of that majestic robe !

Lord of the lordly sea,

Earth's mightiest sailor he :

   Great Captain among them,

     The captors of the globe.

When shall the world forget

Thy glory and our debt,

Indomitable soul,

Immortal Genoese?

Not while the shrewd salt gale

Whines amid shroud and sail,

Above the rhythmic roll

And thunder of the seas.

THE END

Printed by R. & R. Clark, Edinburgh

www.ingramcontent.com/pod-product-compliance
Lightning Source LLC
Chambersburg PA
CBHW021424090426
42742CB00009B/1251